PRAISE FOR *A Working Girl Can't Win*
BY DEBORAH GARRISON

"*A wonderful collection, full of candor, bereft of b.s. It will speak both to women and to those hunting for clues to same.*"
— NEWSWEEK

"*A trimph of wit and modesty.*"
— THE NEW YORKER

"*Impressive for its variety, concision and sureness of touch. . . . A redemptive poet, and a highly personal one in the best sense. . . . An intense, intelligent and wonderfully sly book of poems that should appeal as much to the general reader as to the poetry devotee. . . . However emphatically this particular working girl tells us she can't win, she can certainly write.*"
— THE NEW YORK TIMES BOOK REVIEW

"*Airy, appealing. . . . Sweet and refreshing.*"
— TIME

"*With their short lines, sneaky rhymes, and casual leaps of metaphor, Garrison's poems have a Dickinsonian intensity, and the Amherst recluse's air of independent-minded, lightly populated singleness. Many a working girl will recognize herself in the poems' running heroine, and male readers will part with her company reluctantly.*"
— JOHN UPDIKE

"*Wry, sexy, appealing . . . with a wonderful lyric candor.*"
— ELLE

"Both accessible and good. . . . neither indecipherable nor simplistic. . . . Gentle."
—DAILY NEWS

"An easy-to-relate-to story of a young woman struggling to find pleasure amid the daily grind of the city. Garrison's triumph has to do not only with her use of language and imagery, but with the ways in which she brings poetry into contemporary life, and vice versa."
—INTERVIEW

"Compelling."
—VOGUE

"Smart. . . . Deborah Garrison manages to present those women who wear black, drink espresso and stay up all night anguishing over the everyday events of life as she evokes their triumphs, successes and fears with grace and wit."
—CHICAGO TRIBUNE

"With blunt punches and wry musings, this small, highly charged book of poems reflects a young woman's struggles in career and marriage."
—CINCINNATI ENQUIRER

"By turns wry and lyrical, they spring with perfect rhythm, yet maintain a quiet elegance. . . . The best ones will pull readers into Garrison's world at warp speed and keep them there for days."
—BOSTON PHOENIX

A Working Girl Can't Win

Deborah Garrison

A Working Girl Can't Win

and Other Poems

The Modern Library
New York

2000 Modern Library Paperback Edition

Grateful acknowledgment is made to *The New Yorker*, in which many of
these poems first appeared, and to *Elle*, *The New York Times*, *Open City*,
and *Slate*, where others were previously published.

Special thanks to Irving Penn for permission to use
his photograph on the front of the jacket.

Library of Congress Cataloging-in-Publication Data
Garrison, Deborah.
    A working girl can't win and other poems / Deborah Garrison.—
2000 Modern Library ed.
     p.   cm.
   ISBN 0-375-75540-3 (alk. paper)
   1. Young women—New York (State)—New York Poetry.
 2. Women—Employment—New York (State)—New York Poetry.
 3. City and town life—New York (State)—New York Poetry.   I. Title.
[PS3557.A734W67   2000]
811'.54—dc21   99-37413

Modern Library website address: modernlibrary.com

Printed in the United States of America

2 4 6 8 9 7 5 3 1

Book design by Tanya Pérez-Rock

For my mother,
and in memory of my father

Contents

Saying Yes to a Drink   3
She is young, and dreams of giving herself over.

Father, R.I.P., Sums Me Up at Twenty-Three   5
She is critiqued from beyond.

Long Weekend at Your House   6
Sometimes female friendship is truest.

November on Her Way   8
She professes renewed passion against the coming chill.

She Was Waiting to Be Told   10
Her heart revealed to him, at least in part.

She Thinks of Him on Her Birthday   12
In which she recalls her father and forgives herself.

An Idle Thought   14
Married at twenty-one, and her mind may wander—

On the Road to Getting You   16
but she invariably returns to their inverted passion.

The Firemen   18
A love poem to nobody in particular;

3:00 A.M. Comedy   20
to her husband asleep;

The Boss   22
to an older man whose kind regard was itself a form of love.

A Working Girl Can't Win   24
She takes notes as another of her sex is condemned.

The Widow's Sex Life   26
Her mother's lot.

I Answer Your Question with a Question   28
Here we go again (again);

You Prune Your List in Summer   30
*and again love doesn't go as planned, yet there is perverse
consolation in solitude.*

Her Majesty Loses Her Touch   33
She lies awake feeling older but not necessarily wiser;

Maybe There's No Going Back   35
*and despairs of taking passion seriously, now she sees herself
clearly.*

Please Fire Me   37
The desire for oblivion runs high at the office.

Superior   39
She is rude and subversive, but holds her tongue.

Fight Song   41
She may have the last word yet.

The Warning   43
A letter (undelivered) to a man she might have known better.

Happily Married   46
A confluence.

Perfectionist on the Beach   48
Her oldest friend can still disturb her mind.

Atlantic Wind   51
The mischief in the air seeps into her.

A Friendship Enters Phase II   54
Her newest friend turns the night inside out.

A Kiss   56
in memory speaks volumes.

Husband, Not at Home   58
A different kind of adoration.

Worked Late on a Tuesday Night   60
Not the beginning of the end but the end of the beginning.

A Working Girl Can't Win

Saying Yes to a Drink

What would a grown woman do?
She'd tug off an earring
when the phone rang, drop it to the desk

for the clatter and roll. You'd hear
in this the ice, tangling in the glass;
in her voice, low on the line, the drink

being poured. All night awake,
I heard its fruity murmur of disease
and cure. I heard the sweet word "sleep,"

which made me thirstier. Did I say it,
or did you? And will I learn
to wave the drink with a good-bye wrist

in conversation, toss it off all bracelet-bare
like more small talk about a small affair?
To begin, I'll claim what I want

is small: the childish hand
of a dream to smooth me over,
a cold sip of water in bed,

your one kiss, never again.
I'll claim I was a girl before this gin,
then beg you for another.

Father, R.I.P., Sums Me Up at Twenty-Three

She has no head for politics,
craves good jewelry, trusts too readily,

marries too early. Then
one by one she sends away her friends

and stands apart, smug sapphire,
her answer to everything a slender

zero, a silent shrug—and every day
still hears me say she'll never be pretty.

Instead she reads novels, instead her belt
matches her shoes. She is master

of the condolence letter, and knows
how to please a man with her mouth:

Good. Nose too large, eyes too closely set,
hair not glorious blonde, not her mother's red,

nor the glossy black her younger sister has,
the little raven I loved best.

Long Weekend at Your House

Strands of wind move
through your house
like the finest blonde hair,
like your hair.

The porch that needs painting
peels its white skin in the sun.
We eat breakfast out here, although
it is nearly fall, and too cold.

You've spent a score of summers
slipping out this screen door
which sighs *No* when opened,
Yes when closed—out to town

or the sea, alone.
The caretaker lives
in the potting shed,
a fair-skinned man with slender hands;

he parks his spindly bike
against the gate, sketches,
fries his breakfast
in the kitchen's best iron skillet.

Together, we envy him.
From his garden we pilfer
the last tomatoes of August.
We bite into them like peaches.

But it's September, and you tell me
how few men you've loved.
Outside, you point at the scrubby pine,
the path to a cliff,

the fading rug of summertime.
All this you are heir to.
Of course I want to be you.
Inside, the brown spines of books

your parents must have read
in their stormiest season.
At night I sink into their bed
and sleep.

November on Her Way

Here we go again,
up the narrow stair
of fall, and I'm full of nerve,

have to have you, I'm looking for you
everywhere. It's true
I like men too much, and when

I see one in the street
I used to know—starting to be
bald, in a raincoat eight years old,

worry a lit fish swimming across
his face—I could nearly wrap myself
around him, I'm all too ready. . . .

But I'm sorry! It was for you
I meant to do these things, for you
to unbutton my blouse without a care—

Not so difficult, now the sun is tart,
the river the very color of cold,
November on her way to winter.

She Was Waiting to Be Told

For you she learned to wear a short black slip
and red lipstick,
how to order a glass of red wine
and finish it. She learned to reach out
as if to touch your arm and then not
touch it, changing the subject.
Didn't you think, she'd begin, or
Weren't you sorry. . . .

To call your best friends
by their schoolboy names
and give them kisses good-bye,
to look away when they say
Your wife! So your confidence grows.
She doesn't ask what you want
because she knows.

Isn't that what you think?

When actually she was only waiting
to be told *Take off your dress*—
to be stunned, and then do this,
never rehearsed, but perfectly obvious:

---

in one motion up, over, and gone,
the X of her arms crossing and uncrossing,
her face flashing away from you in the fabric
so that you couldn't say if she was
appearing or disappearing.

She Thinks of Him on Her Birthday

It's still winter,
and still I don't know you
anymore, and you don't know

me. But this morning I stand
in the kitchen with the illusion,
peeling a clementine. Each piece

snaps like the nickname for a girl,
the tinny bite it was
to be one once. Again I count

your daughters and find myself in the middle,
the waist of the hourglass,
endlessly passed through and passed through

but holding nothing, dismayed
by the grubby February sun
I was born under and the cheap pleasure

it gives the window. Yet I raise the shade
for it, and try not to feel it is wrong
to want spring, to be a season

further from you—not wrong to wish
for a hard rain, a hard wind
like one we sat out in together
or came in from together.

An Idle Thought

I'm never going to sleep
with Martin Amis
or anyone famous.
At twenty-one I scotched
my chance to be
one of the seductresses
of the century,
a vamp on the rise through the ranks
of literary Gods and military men,
who wouldn't stop at the President:
she'd take the Pentagon by storm
in halter dress and rhinestone extras,
letting fly the breasts that shatter
crystal—then dump him, too,
and break his power-broker heart.

Such women are a breed apart.
I'm the type
who likes to cook—no,
really likes it; does the bills;
buys towels and ties;
closes her eyes during kisses:
a true first wife.

The seductress when she's fifty
nobody misses, but a first wife
always knows she's first,
and the second (if he leaves me
when he's forty-five) won't forget me
either. The mention of my name,
the sight of our son—his and mine—
will make her tense; despite
perfected bod, highlighted hair
and hip career, she'll always fear
that way back there
he loved me more
and better simply
for being first.

But ho:
the fantasy's unfair to him,
who picked me young and never tried
another. The only woman he's ever left
was his mother.

On the Road to Getting You

Lately I can't help wanting us
to be like other people.
For example, if I were a smoker,

you'd lift a match to the cigarette
just as I put it between my lips.
It's never been like that

between us: none of that
easy chemistry, no quick, half automatic
flares. Everything between us

had to be learned.
Saturday finds me brooding
behind my book, all my fantasies

of seduction run up
against the rocks.
Tell me again

why you don't like
sex in the afternoon?
No, don't tell me—

———

I'll never understand you,
never understand us, America's strangest
loving couple: they never

drink a bottle of wine together,
and rarely look at each other.
Into each other's eyes, I mean.

It's true: never across the dinner table
does he give her that look,
the stock-in-trade of husbands

everywhere, the one that says
he wants to go home to bed.
And when they get there—

when I get you in my arms
I turn my face
to the side so as not

to catch you out, you
always the last to know
about your own passion.

———

The Firemen

God forgive me—

It's the firemen,
leaning in the firehouse garage
with their sleeves rolled up
on the hottest day of the year.

As usual, the darkest one is handsomest.
The oldest is handsomest.
The one with the thin, wiry arms is handsomest.
The young one already going bald is handsomest.

And so on.
Every day I pass them at their station:
the word sexy wouldn't do them justice.
Such idle men are divine—

especially in summer, when my hair
sticks to the back of my neck,
a dirty wind from the subway grate
blows my skirt up, and I feel vulgar,

lifting my hair, gathering it together,
tying it back while they watch
as a kind of relief.
Once, one of them walked beside me

to the corner. Looked into my eyes.
He said, "Will I never see you again?"
Gutsy, I thought.
I'm afraid not, I thought.

What I said was *I'm sorry.*
But how could he look into my eyes
if I didn't look equally into his?
I'm sorry: as though he'd come close, as though

this really were a near miss.

3:00 A.M. Comedy

Sometimes it's funny, this after-hour when
whatever hasn't happened between us
hasn't happened again, and I pretend

to be another kind of woman, who spends
the night on the couch in a rage,
on strike for affection—

How ridiculous.
I'm always in this bed,
if not having you, then forgiving you

exquisitely, consoling myself
with a lame joke: I'm a shrinking
being, tinier and tinier I grow,

there I go!
The last woman on earth
who even bothered about sex,

and now I'm nothing but a speck.
What a shame for all those lusty men;
their world without me is barren.

———

While you, my dear, get
larger: you're a hulking, man-
shaped continent, a cool green

giant (I can hardly reach your leafy
parts), or a statuesque
philosopher-king, whose sleep soars

above mathematics, his loftiest argument.

The Boss

A firecracker, even after middle age
set in, a prince of repression
in his coat and tie, with cynical words

for everything dear to him.
Once I saw a snapshot of the house
he lives in, its fence painted

white, the flowers a wife
had planted leaning into the frame
on skinny stalks, shaking little pom-poms

of color, the dazzle all
accidental, and I felt
a hot, corrective

sting: our lives would never
intersect. At some point
he got older, trimmer, became

the formidable man around the office.
His bearing upright, what hair he has
silver and smooth, he shadows my doorway,

jostling the change in his pocket—
milder now, and mildly vexed.
The other day he asked what on earth

was wrong with me, and sat me down
on his big couch, where I cried
for twenty minutes straight,

snuffling, my eyeliner
betraying itself in the stained
tears. Impossible to say I was crying

because he had asked. He passed
tissues, at ease with the fearsome
womanly squall that made me alien

even to myself. No, it didn't make him
squirm. Across his seventy years,
over his glasses, he eyed me kindly,

and I thought what countless scenes
of tears, of love revealed,
he must have known.

A Working Girl Can't Win

Is this the birth of a pundit
or a slut? Is she the woman
they courted for her youthful edge
or a kiss-and-tell bimbo,
a careerist coquette?
The loyal daughter to spin doctors
losing their hair or soul sister
to feminist essayists everywhere?
Is her meteoric rise the source
of her potential demise?
Is her worldview equal parts
yuppie whine and new-age rumor?
Can we get a biopsy on her latest
breast tumor? Is she a failed
anorexic, or diet-pill faddist
who'll let it all go and get fat
in her fifties? Are her roots
rural, right-leaning? Is she Jewish,
self-hating? Past her sell-by date,
or still ovulating?
Will her husband talk?
Does he mind her success?
Does anyone know—does he see

her undressed? Has she been
photographed? Will she play
truth or dare? And more to the point,
does anyone care?
Come next year, will the masses
be reading her story? Will she be
on the cover, or well past her glory?
Either way, we'll move on, and she'll tire
before long: only her children will grieve
at the way she was wronged.

The Widow's Sex Life

Two summers after he died, it began.
She had coffee with a man
from the other side of the tracks:
he'd been in the navy, worked on the line
at the auto plant.
We hated his hick talk:
"So I says to her, I says . . ."
He'd never read a book!
Now she'd pay for raising snobs.
My sister was still young enough to cry,
to slam her bedroom door
and rage for the ironical ghost of our father.

Poor Mother.
We didn't make it easy for her.
She couldn't spend a night away:
had to share her car with teenagers
and cook our dinner, too; hide in Father's den
to use the phone. Wonder what she whispered there:
was it love, or some other kind of care?

They planted a garden at his place,
baked loaves of bread, watched TV,

and went to bed weekly.
Did everything but
move in together.
And marry: she wouldn't have him.

Was it because we wouldn't let her?
In any case he cheated on her, and she
(just as we'd said) deserved better.

I Answer Your Question with a Question

Don't ask me so soon
when I'm going to leave you.
It's only mid-June, a few more weeks

of peonies yet. I used to hate
their furry scent, their fat cheeks packed
with held breath, the way they'd crumple open

later, like women in tears.
Now I insist I'll never grow sick of them.
So I'm extravagant!

Here: stand over this vase.
Do you call the dipping in your gut
happiness? Do the letters of my name

go loose in your mouth, all salt
and silver, too strange to spell me?
Am I perfectly clear to you now,

am I abstract?
Tell me it isn't marvelous.
Or do you think it's just this

brief confusion in the foyer,
these giddy flowers?

You Prune Your List in Summer

Where I am the sky has been trying
to clear all morning.
At noon the sea is sparking
green, a giant coin flipped and

falling, and there are warnings:
a plane towing an ad for cigarettes
(pleasures are dangerous),
the sun's fuzzy mouth sucking the day back

in through the haze.
I am in search of the perfect stone
for you—as if it would help!
What good are stones to you

now, rose or black,
pointed, smooth?
Why remind you? Why be
heavy in your hand?

Where you are—
the truth is I don't know
where you are.
Maybe the city:

lunch date with a noisy woman,
rainstorm, the umbrella forgotten.
And more phone messages!
All afternoon you prune your list,

and I can see you crossing us off,
peeling back layers, working
down to the ribbed, worn
pit of your self, then

setting out, tons lighter,
like the prow of a boat without
its boat behind, and ladyless
in front: no more breasts to the wind,

no more long, carved hair.
Don't worry. Already it's weeks
I lie in bed mourning your loss,
already I remember this summer

like a summer gone, and myself
like a woman who rented here years ago—
her radio and sunscreen, her stack
of paperbacks. It was she

———

paddling the warm wave of getting away,
she slender, on a diet from love,
who was free. Free!
Best self, lost sister, I start

to forget her, wondering
if at the corner of your day
my colors don't still go up,
a small disturbance, a tat of flag

nicking the morning at the edge of your view.

Her Majesty Loses Her Touch

Back in the days
when I was called Queen of Cherries
I used to write.
Not like this.
I'd lie in bed at night
composing bawdy lyrics,
a regal drifter through my private orchard
of no regrets.
Cherries simply rained
down on my head.

Was I grateful?
Not really.
I was entertained.
And comforted
by the idea that I was only
taking what had been given me.
I committed a thousand acts of love nightly
and didn't notice that in the morning
I was happy.

Now when I close my eyes I see her
dwarfed, jigging out her misery

———

under a barren tree—a sexless jester
she, who once reigned supreme
among bushels and pits,
who sang of mischief from the high, fragrant
branches!
Poetic justice.
I'd laugh, too, if I weren't
so desperate.

Maybe There's No Going Back

Used to be he
was my heart's desire.
His forthright gaze,
his expert hands:

I'd lie on the couch with my eyes
closed just thinking about it.
Never about the fact
that everything changes,

that even this,
my best passion,
would not be immune.
No, I would bask on in an

eternal daydream of the hands
finding me, the gaze like a winding
stair coaxing me down. . . .
Until I caught a glimpse

of something in the mirror:
silly girl in her lingerie,
dancing with the furniture—
a hot little bundle, flush with

clichés. Into that pair
of too-bright eyes I looked
and saw myself. And something else:
he would never look that way.

Please Fire Me

Here comes another alpha male,
and all the other alphas
are snorting and pawing,
kicking up puffs of acrid dust

while the silly little hens
clatter back and forth
on quivering claws and raise
a titter about the fuss.

Here comes another alpha male—
a man's man, a dealmaker,
holds tanks of liquor,
charms them pantsless at lunch:

I've never been sicker.
Do I have to stare into his eyes
and sympathize? If I want my job
I do. Well I think I'm through

with the working world,
through with warming eggs
and being Zenlike in my detachment
from all things Ego.

I'd like to go
somewhere else entirely,
and I don't mean
Europe.

Superior

She came to dread the way he would wander
into her office, his eyes flicking over the papers
on her desk as though it offended him
to have to interrupt tasks that were being done
for him, as though the details she was mistress of
would needlessly clutter his manager's mind.
As he talked of the Big Picture, of who was soon
to die and who to win a prize, the pencil
she held poised a few inches above the text
she'd been correcting when he breezed in
was her only protest. Did it irk him—
the way she kept her shoulders slightly rounded
over the page, the way the graphite stub in her smudged
fingers accused him?

Probably not, as he warmed to his speech;
he was a thinker-aloud, couldn't have a thought
unless he spoke it out before an obedient listener.
She saw the air thronged with his conceptual
offspring; if she didn't keep her slack mouth shut
(now he paused, mid-phrase, touching the air
with an index finger just where he saw
his point appear), she might actually swallow

one of his soap bubbles, like a cartoon character
sucking her whole 2-D world
back down. He talked on.

She agreed, she agreed, she seconded his thesis,
and with each murmured yes her certainty mounted:
she would never be one of them—a Director, a Manager,
an Executive Thingy. She didn't have the ambition.
She was simply a pencil, scratching, pausing,
picking her way down an obscure page.
She liked her fate.
But would she be left alone to enjoy it?
He hovered there—couldn't bear to release her—
now about to turn and go—but no.
He was settling in her single chair and leaning near
to confide more fully in her.

Fight Song

Sometimes you have to say it:
Fuck them all.

Yes fuck them all—
the artsy posers,
the office blowhards
and brown-nosers;

Fuck the type who gets the job done
and the type who stands on principle;
the down-to-earth and understated;
the overhyped and underrated;

Project director?
Get a bullshit detector.

Client's mum?
Up your bum.

You can't be nice to everyone.

When your back is to the wall
When they don't return your call

When you're sick of saving face
When you're screwed in any case

Fuck culture scanners, contest winners,
subtle thinkers and the hacks who offend them;
people who give catered dinners
and (saddest of sinners) the sheep who attend them—

which is to say fuck yourself
and the person you were: polite and mature,
a trooper for good. The beauty is
they'll soon forget you

and if they don't
they probably should.

The Warning

I found out, by accident, about
something you'd done to your wife,
soon to be ex.

You raged at me,
said a lot of things
you didn't mean, like
"All men are shits. Women
just have to deal with it."
I said, "This isn't the worst crime
mankind has been known to commit."
You told me if I ever breathed a word—
as though I would!

You wouldn't remember,
but you were a glamorous figure,
the beleaguered young father,
telling me at the coffee machine
that we twenty-four-year-olds had *no idea. . . .*
You were only thirty-six.
But that was old to me then.
Once you told me about your tenth
anniversary: walking home from dinner

together, you'd reflected that the marriage
was dead. Didn't like each other
one bit, or so you said
you'd said.

I remember telling my husband about it
in bed. What was he trying to prove?
he asked. I wondered, too,
but you stayed in my head—
baring the tarnished honors
of your sexual rank to instruct me,
and the picture of you and her
not holding hands, discussing
your mutual dislike like a savings bond
you'd cash in if things
got worse. It was the kind of uncalled-for
honesty that's nearly antisocial,
but momentarily seems the only thing
that's real—you know, fuck the rest
of them who never say what they truly feel.

A critique of conversation between
men and women, a token

of adult respect:
you couldn't know how I clung to it,
replaying it mentally on our anniversaries,
silently thanking you
when it wasn't true of us yet.

Happily Married

Almost home
on the longest day of the year,
I saw two birds on a telephone wire:
two beaks, two sharp-peaked ruffs,
two tails that stuck down stiff
like two closed fans
all matched up neatly,
and against the faintly
yellow pre-dusk sky
the birds and wire
were all one color,
a fading black
or darkening gray.

Sometimes the smallest thing
brings harmony in
through the eye.
Or was it that I
on that particular day
had harmony to bring
to what I saw?
That I'd even looked up
seemed a piece of marital

good luck, and that they didn't
move as I passed by—

I wondered how long in fact
they'd sit that way.

Perfectionist on the Beach

Eighty-six degrees, high tide.
We were arguing about suicide.
Me, safe from sun under the umbrella;
you, propped on your elbows in the sand,
your arms, recently iron-pumped, bronzing smoothly,
your short gold curls and strong nose almost
Roman coinworthy as you scanned
the water with restless air and announced
you'd kill yourself, you really would,
if you weren't a coward.
While I maintained the wish to die
itself was cowardly.
And I didn't believe you:
you didn't really want to die.
What about speed and wind—
your long bike rides, tracing the harbor
on unknown roads? What about your pencil
setting a line on a clean sheet of drafting
paper? Women with small breasts
and certain customs you were said
to love in bed? At the very least,
the kind of happiness that's purely physical.

The person who wants to die,
you snapped, doesn't care about
any of that. He'd give it all up
for a moment's peace. Peace from
striving, from endless dissatisfaction
with a self that's less than ideal.
I'd do it, you insisted, if I weren't
shit-scared of pain.

If it's pain you don't like
you'd take pills, I said.
But I hadn't won, and added lamely,
Aren't you curious how your life
is going to Turn Out? That's not
a question of being brave—
only mildly vain, which you are,
or so you claim.

You didn't answer for a while,
and half-enraged (or was it half in love)
I watched your critic's eye alight

on a black-haired figure clad in white
bikini as she ran lightly down
the hard-packed sand and dove
into a creamy wave.

Atlantic Wind

Up out of the surf
like a dog gone swimming,
slagging sand and spray every which way

and making the news unreadable.
Nosing its cloud-pups across
the sun so that no one can tell

if the afternoon is hot or cool.
First sun, then no sun;
then with silent roar the sun again

as this restive breath uproots
the gay umbrellas and sends them
crashing down the beach, flowers become

missiles. I'm trying to nap,
the towel slapping jiblike
at my legs, the hat that wants

to fly pinned over my cheeks
with a crooked elbow—don't know
if I'm frying or chilled as I descend

---

in my dream a hill
where every headstone tilts,
where the grasses bow down obedient

to the blast, and the flowers bow down
too, or are uprooted like more wayward
umbrellas, flung up into the tossing

sky, and then down again spinning
they come, now small black
parachutes plummeting soundlessly

and from their strings dangle
a hundred men, dropped into a war
and sure to meet their deaths,

their hundred fates so many bits
of seed or spore, their names
I struggle against sleep to know

but nameless they drop
and someone says we'll never
see them more. . . .

Dream over. One eye
open, I spy the rustling
scene askew: a wailing baby

smacks the sand with one small hand;
a girl smooches her guy, a cord of hair
whipping round his neck in the horny

breeze. Oh me oh my a golden noose
to cinch the kiss: why does the world
sometimes menace us like this?

The wind can't tell you,
nor can the poets, all along
the seaside road come out

on battered porches
with their typewriters, thinking
to tap their souls away in the fury

but the paper won't stay put.

———

A Friendship Enters Phase II

We were sitting on the porch
after dinner, grown-ups taking
stock, no chance of our stopping:

we were going to stay up all night.
"We're going to stay up all night,"
one of us said, and you lit another cigarette

with a lazy flair,
like we'd just been in bed,
but our love was pure; I'd never

talked like that to anyone before.
Two fathers, one husband,
three would-be lovers were duly sworn

and testified before us in their turn;
their crimes were numerous;
when we peered down their gun barrels

their faces and hands and eyes glinted
and winked maddeningly at the other end.
And we were mad—mad to shake the kaleidoscope

again: even virginity, that shoeless waif,
streaked low across the moonless cloudlake like
a slip blown from the line and carried off

to rest in some stranger's muddy yard.
All, please: we'd tell no less, no stone
was left, etc. . . . . You were the maestro,

twirling a smoke in the dark,
then piping on it, braving the toy
puffs of death, conducting the ragtag band

of losses. "But why," you asked,
"didn't he love *me?*" Your deep laugh
dissolved into the peopled space between

the summer trees, whose black leaves flickered green
as morning came—the bitch!—to shut us down.
Good-bye, perfect night. You raised

your empty dinner glass to toast
our forward march, and tossing back
invisible shots we proceeded
backward into the light.

———

A Kiss

It was not like everyone had said.
Not like being needed,
or needing; not desperate;
it did not whisper
that I'd come to harm. I didn't lose

my head. No, I was not
going to leap from a great
height and flap
my wings.
It was in fact

the opposite of flying:
it contained the wish
to be toppled, to be on the floor,
the ground, anywhere I might
lie down. . . .

On my back, and you on me.
Do you mind?
Not like having a conversation, exactly,
though not unlike telling
and being told—

What?
That I was like a woman admitting
there was a part of herself she didn't know?
There was a part of myself.
I didn't know.

An introduction,
then, to the woman I was like,
at least as long as you kissed me.
Now that's a long time,
at least a couple of women ago.

Husband, Not at Home

A soldier, a soldier,
gone to the litigation wars,

or down to Myrtle Beach
to play golf with Dad for the weekend.

Why does the picture of him
tramping the emerald grass in those

silly shoes or flinging his tie over his shoulder
to eat a take-out dinner at his desk—

the carton a squat pagoda in the forest
of legal pads on which he drafts,

in all block caps, every other line,
his motions and replies—fill her

with obscure delight?
Must be the strangeness: his life

strange to her, and hers to him,
as she prowls the apartment with a vacuum

in boxers (his) and bra, or flings
herself across the bed

with three novels to choose from
in the delicious, sports-free

silence. Her dinner a bowl
of cereal, taken cranelike, on one

leg, hip snug to the kitchen
counter. It makes her smile to think

he'd disapprove, to think she likes him
almost best this way: away.

She'll let the cat jump up
to lap the extra milk, and no one's

home to scold her.

Worked Late on a Tuesday Night

Again.
Midtown is blasted out and silent,
drained of the crowd and its doggy day.
I trample the scraps of deli lunches
some ate outdoors as they stared dumbly
or hooted at us career girls—the haggard
beauties, the vivid can-dos, open raincoats aflap
in the March wind as we crossed to and fro
in front of the Public Library.

Never thought you'd be one of them,
did you, little lady?
Little Miss Phi Beta Kappa,
with your closetful of pleated
skirts, twenty-nine till death do us
part! Don't you see?
The good schoolgirl turns thirty,
forty, singing the song of time management
all day long, lugging the briefcase

home. So at 10:00 PM
you're standing here
with your hand in the air,

cold but too stubborn to reach
into your pocket for a glove, cursing
the freezing rain as though it were
your difficulty. It's pathetic,
and nobody's fault but
your own. Now

the tears,
down into the collar.
Cabs, cabs, but none for hire.
I haven't had dinner; I'm not half
of what I meant to be.
Among other things, the mother
of three. Too tired, tonight,
to seduce the father.

About the Author

DEBORAH GARRISON was born in Ann Arbor. In 1986 she joined the editorial staff of *The New Yorker,* where she is currently a senior editor. Her poetry began appearing in *The New Yorker* and elsewhere in 1987. She lives with her husband in Manhattan.

About the Type

The text of this book was set in Palatino, designed by the German typographer Hermann Zapf. It was named after the Renaissance calligrapher Giovanbattista Palatino. Zapf designed it between 1948 and 1952, and it was his first typeface to be introduced in America.